TAKE A KNEE

★ TIME OUT TO LOOK UP ★

A 30-Day Devotional Journey

by CH (BG) Charles "Ray" Bailey
U.S. Army, Retired

ARMED ★ SERVICES
MINISTRY
AMERICAN BIBLE SOCIETY

TAKE A KNEE
TIME OUT TO LOOK UP

All Scripture quotations are fully cited from the Common English Bible, English Standard Version, Good News Translation, New English Translation, New Living Translation and The Message.

Armed Services Ministry™ is a subsidiary and trademark of American Bible Society. All other trademarks are property of their respective owners.

The views expressed in this book are solely those of the author and do not necessarily reflect any views and opinions of the Department of Defense or its components.

Edited by:
Chaplain (COL) Arthur C. Pace, Retired
LTC Richard Braud, Retired
Chaplain (CPT) David S. Keller
Annie LoCastro
Stacey L. Wright

Design by:
Caleb Komorowski

ABS Item #124426
ISBN 9781941449974

Printed in the United States of America

FORWARD

I called this book *Take a Knee, Time Out to Look Up* to encourage the reader to make time each day for the Lord. Each of us needs to take a knee, as it were, in the busyness of our day to spend time with God in personal prayer and Bible study. This discipline is important to me, and gave rise to my writing these devotionals.

I began to write these devotionals in 1996, which I called, "Reunion Tidbits." I sent them to the staff of my unit in preparation for our re-deployment from Bosnia. After being deployed for a year, I wanted the troops to have some support for their reunion with family and friends.

When we returned, I announced that I would stop writing them. I was overwhelmed with requests to continue these encouraging messages. One person told me, "It is the only positive email I get all day and I look forward to it." Since then, I have continued to write these thoughts. Thanks in part to email, my audience has grown significantly. I have received many warm comments on the impact these devotionals have had on the lives of my readers.

I truly feel blessed to be able to share my daily thoughts with you. They are written as part of my daily devotionals and I am allowing you to "overhear" my thoughts.

I wish to thank my Lord and Savior Jesus Christ, who inspires me, my wonderful family who gave me support (and sometimes topics to write about), and my friends who encouraged me to continue when I felt I had run out of things to say. By taking time each day to read these, I hope you will be encouraged in your Christian walk, challenged to achieve your fullest faith potential, and inspired to live a life that is in complete trust and obedience to our loving God and his Holy Word.

Charlie "Ray" Bailey

CONTENTS

TAKE A KNEE

OUR SCRIPTURE: *"As soon as Solomon finished praying and making these requests to the Lord, he got up from before the Lord's altar, where he had been kneeling with his hands spread out to heaven." – 1 Kings 8:54 (Common English Bible)*

It's a scorching mid-August day. The heat blazes, humidity clings and sweat bleeds as we run and march, endure excruciating push-ups and parachute landing falls. You know the drill. We're black and blue. There are no breaks. Attrition is high as student after student fails, or falls out; our class steadily dwindles. Morale sinks. We doubt it's worth it. Will we ever make it through? It's a tough training day at airborne school, Fort Benning, Georgia.

The "black hat" NCO instructor abruptly stops the training, telling all of us to gather under a shade tree. In a strong voice, he barks, "Take a knee!" We're shocked, but relieved, to stop for any reason. We wonder about the lecture and how we had messed up. Instead, the instructor looks into our faces and begins to ask how we are doing. He asks about our families. Have we called them? Did we write? He asks if we have been getting enough rest. Have we eaten properly to keep up our strength? He picks out several Soldiers and individually asks if we have been taking care of our feet. Do we have any blisters? When was the last time we spoke to our sweetheart? And, do we think we can go on?

The shock of such questions is replaced by a strong feeling of being cared for and believed in. We take a deep breath, a sigh of relief, and begin looking deep inside, reflecting on why we're here and what we're doing.

Staring into the sea of faces, he abruptly switches topics, inquiring if it's now worth it and do we have the courage and faith to go on. With a resounding unified voice, we affirm our willingness to persevere. As a smile slowly forms, he then says he believes we can, but we have to keep our life in balance and take care of ourselves.

Continued on next page.

TAKE A KNEE

I remember that day so vividly, and its memory is now woven into another aspect of how I should keep my life balanced, strong, and ready to serve. Our Creator has given each of us unbelievable capabilities and a lion's heart to go forward. But, constant times come to "take a knee," in personal reflection, and prayer, to see what the Instructor wants us to do. We need to stop, reflect, ask, and readjust our lives to meet life's challenges, especially as we follow and take orders from our Master.

Today, take a knee. Honestly reflect and assess your life. Are you going the right way? Listen to God, who cares deeply about you as you are asked about your soul. Take a knee of faith.

OUR PRAYER: *Master, I get so busy making life complicated. You step in and remind me that life is a gift and is full of simple joys in service of others. Help me to be humble enough to change what needs to be changed. Remind me that it is not too hard. Amen.*

JOY IS NOT THE NAME OF A GIRL

OUR SCRIPTURE: *"He said to them, 'Go and eat delicacies and drink sweet drinks and send portions to those for whom nothing is prepared. For this day is holy to our Lord. Do not grieve, for the joy of the Lord is your strength.'"*
– Nehemiah 8:10 (New English Translation)

Have you ever come to the end of a day, week, or the conclusion of a project and felt emotionally depleted? We've all worn out physically, but I'm talking about a numbness of the spirit. Your inner core is completely depleted and everything seems superficial.

It reminds me of most of my flashlights. When I finally find them, there's a weak light, using the last of their expended battery power. Around this time, my (spirit) battery is so low you must squint to notice if there is any light at all. Lately, I've thought about how to renew my spirit, how to renew my batteries. I need to find my joy.

No, it's not the other woman "Joy," or even the dish washing detergent, but more the joy from the heart: to see life in a bright, dazzling way again.

I am not alone. You and others may be on this same quest. The fatigue of dealing with roles, positions and demands deplete our joy. Six weeks before he died, a reporter asked Elvis Presley, "Elvis, when you first started playing music, you said you wanted to be rich, famous and happy. Are you happy?" "I'm lonely as hell," he replied.

His happiness was dependent upon the wrong things. Elvis, like many of us, wanted happiness in the form of outward gains and accomplishments. Why then do we find this so dissatisfying? Maybe, it is not really happiness that we desire, but joy. Happiness is a temporary emotion; joy is a condition of the soul. Joy, which comes from the Lord, offers contentment in any situation.

Continued on next page.

JOY IS NOT THE NAME OF A GIRL

George Bernard Shaw said it best: "This is the true joy in life, the being used for a purpose recognized by yourself as a mighty one: the being thoroughly worn out before you are thrown on the scrap heap, and being a force of nature instead of a feverish selfish little clod of ailments and grievances, complaining that the world will not devote itself to making you happy." Now, that sure beats despair or misery: the opposites of joy. Even when someone bumps your elbow, and you spill your cup of happiness, you will never lose your joy.

I am discovering that the joy of who I am, in the Lord, is critical to my happiness in what I do. Look today within yourself and check on your spirit. What is the condition of your joy? Does it need to be renewed? No one around you can give you a renewal. It must come from God.

OUR PRAYER: *Master, I am always trying to find joy in things and in people. They all fade away, but you never do. Thank you for being so faithful. Amen.*

OUR SCRIPTURE: *"A time to kill, and a time to heal; a time to break down, and a time to build up; a time to weep, and a time to laugh; a time to mourn, and a time to dance. A time to throw away stones, and a time to gather stones; a time to embrace, and a time to refrain from embracing."*
– Ecclesiastes 3:3-5 (New English Translation)

It's all in the view. If you stand on your head, you see the world upside down. If you lie horizontal, you see things sideways. If you close your eyes, you see the world in darkness and become blind to reality. However, if you stare at the sun, you see things in total brightness, but once again, become blind to reality. Too much of either hides what is real. It's all in the view.

In the same way, an optimist sees the best in the world; while a pessimist sees only the worst. An optimist finds the positive in the negative, and a pessimist only finds the negative in the positive. For example, an avid duck hunter was in the market for a new bird dog. His search ended when he found a dog that could actually walk on water to retrieve a duck. Shocked by his find, he was sure none of his friends would ever believe him. He decided to try to break the news to a friend of his, a pessimist by nature, and invited him to hunt with him and his new dog.

As they waited by the shore, a flock of ducks flew by. They fired, and a duck fell. The dog responded and jumped into the water. The dog, however, did not sink; instead he walked across the water to retrieve the bird, never getting more than his paws wet. This continued all day long; each time a duck fell, the dog walked across the water's surface to retrieve it.

The pessimist watched carefully, saw everything, but did not say a single word. On the drive home, the hunter asked his friend, "Did you notice anything unusual about my new dog?"

Continued on next page.

"I sure did," responded the pessimist. "He can't swim."

Too much of anything is too much. Too many unrealistic views skewer reality. Even too much optimism or pessimism can be blinding. We either refuse to see the good before us or the negative we need to address. We blind ourselves to what is true and real. There needs to be a healthy balance.

But, what is the balance? I think it's knowing when to cry and when to laugh--- and, how much of each. Too much of either one can be blinding. You recognize the negative and handle it with the positive. As Oscar Wilde said before he died, "Either that wallpaper goes, or I do."

The Master gave each of us tears of sadness and joy. Use both to live life in balance.

OUR PRAYER: *Master, keep my life in balance. When life gets uneven, even me out, as only you can. Amen.*

SOMETIMES, SOMEDAY, I KNOW

OUR SCRIPTURE: *"I have come as a light into the world, so that everyone who believes in me should not remain in darkness."*
– John 12:46 (New English Translation)

Sometimes…

- There is peace that can be felt.
- There is a joy in pain.
- There is a rainbow in a storm.
- There is a smile in a frown.
- There is laughter in a cry.

Someday…

- The kids will be gone.
- The job will be no more.
- The aching joints will be more.
- There will be goals unmet.
- The days will seem shorter.

I Know…

- There is hope in every situation.
- There is a prayer in everything.
- I will never be alone.
- I will always be loved.
- This moment is more important than lost moments in the past and moments hoped for in the future.
- I am forgiven.

OUR PRAYER: *Master, life changes even when I don't plan on it. Both good and bad are part of these changes. Strengthen my hope and faith in you for only you can always be depended upon. Amen.*

OUR SCRIPTURE: *"Now, O Lord my God, you have made your servant king in my father David's place, even though I am only a young man and am inexperienced."*
– 1 Kings 3:7 (New English Translation)

I read recently about an experiment involving physical education students. Twenty of them were asked to shoot free throws on a basketball court. They practiced twenty minutes a day for twenty days. They improved twenty-four percent.

Twenty other students simply sat in a room, imagining themselves shooting free throws. They imagined stepping up to the free throw line, taking the ball in hand, shooting the ball through the air and dropping it through the hoop. At the end of twenty days, twenty minutes of imagined practice per day, they had the same rate of improvement as the ones who actually shot free throws. Now, that's truly amazing!

Immediately, I began to just imagine going to work, to just imagine exercising, and a whole host of other distasteful duties I would rather do from the comfort of my couch, sipping iced tea. Somehow, I don't think my boss, or my body, would approve or comply.

The point is that our experiences, vividly imagined, have the same impact on our subconscious as experiences we actually live. Our nervous systems can't tell the difference between a real experience and a vividly imagined one. This means our subconscious either works for us or against us.

If you see yourself as a lazy person, then you are. If you see yourself as incompetent, so you shall be. If you see yourself as a failure in work, marriage, parenting, or other roles, you will figure out a way to fail every time. Imagination will win over will power.

Continued on next page.

JUST IMAGINE

The choices of accomplishment and victory are just an imagination away. A stellar achievement, or a "wow" marriage, is ready to be vividly imagined and acted upon. The Lord offers forgiveness, respect, trust, and strength. You just need to imagine, believe---and get off the couch. God imagined outstanding and exciting lives for us. God doesn't make failures.

OUR PRAYER: *Master, I don't have to imagine you love me and will always be by my side. That is an assurance I can stand upon. Amen.*

A LULL IN LIFE

OUR SCRIPTURE: *"O God, you are my God! I long for you! My soul thirsts for you, my flesh yearns for you, in a dry and parched land where there is no water."*
– Psalm 63:1 (New English Translation)

While traveling through several airports, moving from one country to another, and even between several states, I saw the most fascinating human behavior. Two out of every three people had a cell phone up to their ear, making or receiving calls. I even observed when a cell phone rang, several people frantically dove into their purses, or grabbed their phones off their belts to determine if it was their phone that rang. Those who did not receive the call seemed disappointed. Then, I saw the strangest sight of all. A man walking down the hallway, gestured wildly, talking to himself. Upon closer examination, I noticed a strange mechanism behind his ear. I later found out it was a new cell phone gizmo allowing your hands to stay free as you speak.

When people used to act like this, it usually meant they didn't have all their "oars in the water;" they were truly talking to themselves, and sometimes even answering. Those persons used to get pulled off the street for their own safety. Now, it's normal. How can we tell the crazies from the normal people? Maybe, there is no difference, but that's another topic. Anyway, I digress.

It's fascinating how people just "have to have" a cell phone and have to constantly use it. As they sat waiting for a plane, they grew quickly bored and called someone. They couldn't simply sit. As the plane taxied or arrived, they called to keep others current on every phase of the travel. They couldn't just sit there and enjoy the view or moment of solitude. They were almost afraid of the lull in life. Maybe they were lonely or felt isolated and needed to hear a known, caring voice.

I think it's kind of sad. We get so little time to experience solitude and stillness. We seem to search out someone to talk with or something to do to find usefulness and purpose. Maybe, just maybe, others wouldn't mind a break from us; but, we don't like to think about that.

Continued on next page.

A LULL IN LIFE

Without solitude and stillness, we neglect our spirit. Our spirit needs the inner perspective and contemplation without outside influence or competition. In our rushing we leave our spiritual selves behind. Our spirits are drained and confused; we lack identity and direction. Our spirits sustain us for today by anticipating the hope and victory of tomorrow. Without the nourishment and strengthening, our tomorrows become less than hopeful.

Drop the cell phone gizmo off your ear. Reach down and hit the off button. Look out the window and see the wonders and beauty of God's creation. Look at those around you and realize you are different from anyone else and a tomorrow is waiting for you to anticipate.

OUR PRAYER: *Master, silence my thoughts and still my hands and feet. In the quietness, let me hear your still small voice of love. Amen.*

OUR SCRIPTURE: *"If you do this thing, and God so commands you, then you will be able to endure, and all these people will be able to go home satisfied."*
– Exodus 18:23 (New English Translation)

Not wanting to pass the time gazing out a window or at the floor, I read a travel magazine as I flew to my new home away from home. Even though you could say I was traveling, I still felt the irony of reading a travel magazine as I sped across the sky in a C-17 Air Force airplane wearing body armor and a helmet. It was an odd circumstance that only those serving our country could truly understand.

The article was about Australia and the beauty of that country. It's a place I've always wanted to visit. The article spoke of one of Australia's greatest natural attractions, the Great Barrier Reef. Colorful corals stretch hundreds of kilometers along the northern coastline.

At points, it said, you notice the coral in close to the coastline is nowhere near as vibrant and colorful as the coral on the ocean side of the reef. It explained there's a very simple reason for this. The coral on the coastline side is in still water. With no challenge for its survival it dies early. The coral on the ocean side is constantly being tested by wind, waves, and storms - surges of power.

I visualized the difference between these coral formations. As I sat back, I began to consider the article's further implications. The coral with beauty has to fight for survival every day of its life. As it is challenged and tested, it changes and adapts. It grows healthy. It grows strong. And, it reproduces.

Continued on next page.

This is how it is with people, too. Challenged and tested, we come alive. Like coral pounded by the sea, we grow. But, when we lie dormant and untested, in comfort, we lose our strength and beauty. Testing brings out the best, the wonderful colors of our creation within us. Our future meaning and purpose is shaped by our response to hardship and lashing challenges. What we are meant to become is seen through our response to hardship and the challenges lashing against us. We become who God intended us to become.

OUR PRAYER: *Master, allow me to glow and brighten in colors of courage, strength, and humility. Help me to realize all my troubles and challenges will form the person you intended, if I just keep the faith. Amen.*

LOOKING, BUT NOT SEEING

OUR SCRIPTURE: *"Then the Lord opened Balaam's eyes, and he saw the angel of the Lord standing in the way with his sword drawn in his hand; so he bowed his head and threw himself down with his face to the ground."*
– Numbers 22:31 (New English Translation)

We may look and not see. We may walk down the street, in the midst of people with different looks, personalities, experiences, and problems and not see them. That man you just passed was awarded a promotion at work; but, he didn't sleep too well last night because he worried about his daughter's date, and he has a wonderful sense of humor he would love to share. That woman ahead of you is a terrific mother and wife; she's sad because her mother is getting older and needs her, and she wishes she could return to finish her degree. How do we know this? Should we try to know it?

I came across a wonderful quote that read:

> *An interesting thing can be said of us. All of us are watchers — of television, of time clocks, or of traffic on the freeway. But, few are observers. Everyone is looking, not many are seeing.*
>
> – Peter M. Leschak

Yes, we are professional watchers, either through the television lens distancing us from real life, or our car windows as things and people go by in a blur. We even bring our "looking" into our homes, watching and determining issues with our spouse, kids and neighbors. We sigh about "their" issues, pontificating sage advice; but, rarely comforting, keeping our personal distance. We look with our eyes, but we do not see with our hearts. Truly, seeing is to care and get involved.

Have you ever seen a child trying to get your attention because he or she knows you are brushing them off with a casual remark? Do you recall a spouse who knows you are looking at them, but you are not

Continued on next page.

seeing, or understanding, them? How do they know that? Well, you know it in conversations when someone looks right through you, but does not see you.

Today, I challenge you to open your eyes and see. Not the physical eyes of "looking," but the caring eyes of "seeing." Those eyes are clearly in focus. Today, see your wife, or husband, for who they are and why. Today, see your children and their lives in all aspects. Today, see your world in all the ways it is wonderful, and in all the ways it needs your help. Today, gaze into a mirror and truly see yourself. Today is a day to care.

OUR PRAYER: *Master, open my eyes and my heart to the world. Let me truly see what you want me to see, so I may make a difference. Amen.*

THE SHADOW OF FEAR

OUR SCRIPTURE: *"For God did not give us a Spirit of fear but of power and love and self-control."*
– 2 Timothy 1:7 (New English Translation)

It is our single most destructive force and simultaneously successful motivator. It pushes, pulls, and stretches us to heroic acts, as well as cowardly actions. It can lead us to make impulsive or bad decisions, forming some of our greatest regrets. It can also open up the untapped resources of fortitude and power. It's a four letter word you know so well…fear.

We are afraid of failure so we try harder…or, we become passive, and do not try at all. We are afraid of loneliness, so we form relationships, both good and bad. Fear can make you faster, and more accurate in focus, or it can make you fumble with doubt.

It's like the guy who was out of money. He decided to rob the bank because he couldn't think of any other way to get the money. He didn't know anything about robbing banks, so he practiced what he would say over and over. He got a revolver and a sack. Then, he practiced sticking the sack over the counter and pointing the gun in someone's face saying, "Don't mess with me. This is a stick up." When it came time for the real thing, he was really nervous; but, he was confident in his routine.

However, inside the bank, fear took over and he handed the lady the revolver, pointed the sack at her, and said, "Don't stick with me. This is a mess up."

Yes, you could "mess up," but at least you try. Fear is a weapon, and a tool, in our lives. It's the shadow following us to motivate us, or coercing us to give up. It can freeze us up so we do not even attempt anything, or it can make us try harder. It is a flight or fight motivator.

Continued on next page.

THE SHADOW OF FEAR

A football player got to start on the football team his sophomore year. He received the opening kick-off and dropped the ball, picked it up, broke through in the open, and raced down the sidelines with nobody after him. But as he was running, he glanced to his right and saw the shadow of somebody chasing him. He ran faster, but the guy stayed right behind him. He didn't want the guy to catch him so he dove into the end zone. He looked back and there was no one behind him. The shadow he had been running from was his own. Fear will make people run from their own shadow and do foolish things. It can also force us to draw on our inner resources, allowing us to achieve great things.

Fear is normal. You will feel it today in various degrees. It can help you mess up or it can be the shadow that chases you to a touchdown in life.

OUR PRAYER: *Master, I face today with you by my side. I will not fear. Who or what can dare stand against you? Please help me to keep my fear in check and not let it overwhelm me. Amen.*

OUR SCRIPTURE: *"God gave Solomon wisdom and very great discernment; the breadth of his understanding was as infinite as the sand on the seashore."*
– 1 Kings 4:29 (New English Translation)

By my bed is a stack of books. One is the writings of an early Roman Emperor and his philosophical perspectives. It is considered a very enlightening book. Another is a collection of moral discussions on a variety of relevant and critical issues of today. Another is a work of fiction set in the glory of the Old West. I lie there contemplating what to read to enlighten my life. I instinctively pick up the fiction. Yes, I do see the other books. Yes, I do feel a bit guilty for not really getting into the more intellectually, stimulating books. But, allow me to defend myself.

First, I'm tired at night when I finally get to my room. My brain is already frazzled. So, I need to escape to a better place where the good guy wins, gets the girl everyone else wanted, and rides off in the sunset, carefree.

Also, I don't have to think much about what I am reading. It's like watching a movie in my head as I read. When I want to stop, I don't lie awake all night rehashing complex issues. Lastly, it is not dumb reading without any educational purposes of higher learning. I learn a lot. Allow me to expand on this. Here are just a few, mind you, just a few of the highly educational things I have learned and some perspectives that may enlighten you.

1. Never, never sit around a campfire looking into the flames. If Indians, or outlaws, are lying outside in the dark, you will not see them because you are blinded by the fire.

We often blind ourselves to the dangers of our world around us by believing they won't affect us. We think that if we just keep blinders on, then all the bad things will go away. Then, when the dangers do come close, it is now too late. Be alert.

Continued on next page.

2. The best way to teach a lesson to those tempted to rustle cattle is to hang all horse and cow thieves to the nearest tree.

Problems don't go away with apathy. Most of our problems can be solved with aggressive confidence in our abilities to solve and harness issues. Also, if you respond quickly , you may stop other problems that are hiding around the corner.

3. Remember to always leave the trigger of your pistol on an empty chamber. A bullet hole in the foot is painful.

A quick temper can get you into trouble more ways than you can imagine. You tend to shoot off your mouth without aiming your words.

4. If you are a good guy, and a hero, then when you get shot, get stuck in a blizzard, or fall off a tall cliff, someone nice will save your life at the last minute. Most likely, you will wake up with a pretty girl looking at you. The rest you can imagine.

Rewards for being and doing good may sometimes seem slow in coming. Appreciation for good deeds isn't always voiced. This can be discouraging. But, rewards are there. They're not necessarily obvious or immediate. The rewards often come slowly, but are still meaningful. Do good, just for goodness' sake. You will never regret it. You will win in the end, when it counts.

Wisdom comes in all types of packages. The very beginning is the voice of God.

OUR PRAYER: *Master, in all parts of life, both good and bad, I know I can find your wisdom. It is this wisdom that guides me to be better and do better. Your lessons may be rough sometimes, but they are worth learning. Amen.*

BEARING UP UNDER PRESSURE

OUR SCRIPTURE: *"Is it not true that if you do what is right, you will be fine? But if you do not do what is right, sin is crouching at the door. It desires to dominate you, but you must subdue it."*
– Genesis 4:7 (New English Translation)

Allow me to tell you a little story. Hopefully, you will get the moral rather quickly.

A cold winter was just around the corner and a hunter went out, into the forest, to shoot a bear. He planned to make a warm coat. Soon, he saw a big, furry bear coming toward him; he raised his rifle and took aim. "Wait," said the bear, "Why do you want to shoot me?"

"Because I am cold and I need a coat," said the hunter.

"But I am hungry," the bear replied, "so, maybe, if we just talk this over a little, we could come to a compromise."

So, the hunter sat down beside the bear and began to talk over the pros and cons.

In the end, however, the hunter was well enveloped by the bear's fur, and the bear had eaten his dinner.

So often, we face choices in our ethics and morals regarding issues that challenge us. We hold a quick conversation within our minds and hearts rationalizing and debating what is the best choice in light of what is the right choice. We add all kind of tidbits to the equation such as what we deserve, what is fair, what is owed us, what everyone else does which wrestles with what is right, what is truth, what is honorable, and what is ethical and moral. The pros and cons fight it out.

Too often, we rationalize so much that the right and wrong are blurred. We talk our way into what we wanted to do from the beginning, ignoring and shouting over the voice of right and true. The danger is

Continued on next page.

obvious. We get what we selfishly desire, but we lose our integrity and self-respect. We have the warmth of attaining, but we have given up other things much more important such as integrity, an honorable life. We get, but we are also gotten. The good news is that God tells us what is right and true in his holy Word.

OUR PRAYER: *Master, I sometimes confuse what is right and fair, by my agendas and selfishness. But, you have made it clear what is truth. Please help me to accept your truth and stand strong. Amen.*

THE NEED FOR VITAMIN D

OUR SCRIPTURE: *"You are the light of the world. A city set on a hill cannot be hidden. Nor do people light a lamp and put it under a basket, but on a stand, and it gives light to all in the house. In the same way, let your light shine before others, so that they may see your good works and give glory to your Father who is in heaven."* – Matthew 5:14-16 (ESV)

I heard an amusing joke about a young boy in a worship service. During the message, the pastor asked a reflective question to the congregation, "What is a saint?"

The little boy looked up at the great people of faith depicted in the church's stained glass windows and blurted out, "People who let the light shine through!"

This story came to mind when I had just finished an annual physical exam. I came out with flying colors, except for one small glitch in my system. The doctor said I needed more vitamin D. He explained that this wasn't unusual for people who work mostly indoors and are not exposed to sunlight, which is an important source for that vitamin. I saw this as a medical mandate to play more golf or tennis, or to relax in a lounge chair and watch the trees grow. Of course, I ruled out such things as taking out the trash, raking leaves, mowing the lawn or washing the car. What is important, though, is that I needed more natural light in my life.

Both the little boy and the doctor had it right. Not only do we need light to shine upon us and be absorbed, but it also needs to shine through us.

It is easy to live in the darkness of pessimism and cynicism, focusing on the bad things that seem to be all around us. What we need is a light that will shine amid that darkness.

Continued on next page.

THE NEED FOR VITAMIN D

One thing I know is that there is never enough darkness in the entire universe to put out the light of a single candle, as long as it is lit. The same is true with each of us. God's light that radiates from our lives cannot be extinguished by the negative or bleak darkness, unless we lose hope and blow it out for ourselves.

Here is another thought on this subject. You don't have to be the lone light or afraid that your light will not be enough to battle the darkness. No candle loses any of its light when it lights another candle. Just turn to your family member, office worker, or even that person behind the cash register, and light their life's candle with a smile, with respect, and with a word of hope. Let them see the light of Christ shine through you so that they may find their way out of the darkness.

OUR PRAYER: *Master, help me to live in your light, and may your light shine brightly through me. May I encourage others as you have encouraged me. Amen.*

OUR SCRIPTURE: *"...as an inheritance to Israel his servant, for his loyal love endures, to the one who remembered us when we were down, for his loyal love endures, and snatched us away from our enemies, for his loyal love endures."*
– Psalm 136:22-24 (New English Translation)

If you know your western history, money was rare out west. Early Texans made do with trade, barter, and credit. Everyone understood, including preachers and doctors. These professionals received much credit, but not much cash.

Poor pay didn't discourage these professionals. They were rewarded with respect from tough Texans. How did they eat without money? Well, payment came in eggs, chickens, milk, meat, and home-cooked meals.

The story goes that in Big Springs, Texas, a beloved physician died in poverty. He deserved a tombstone worthy of the community's respect. No one had that much money, nor would eggs or chickens pay for it. The cowboys had an idea. They dug up the old hitching post with his weather beaten shingle.

That's how their friend wound up with a fitting memorial and touching epitaph. It was reverently placed on his grave to read as usual:

"DR. JONES – OFFICE UPSTAIRS"

What will people say about you? You may say you really don't care, but that isn't true. We all want to be liked and respected. We want people to be sad when we are gone. We want to leave a good legacy and memory.

What is a main ingredient of being well liked and respected? Simply, it is the influence we had on those around us. Were we perceived as a person who left goodness behind? Did we serve in any capacity,

Continued on next page.

verses seeking only to be served?

Once we leave our role as parent, spouse, boss, friend, or neighbor, what is left? After our outer image fades, what remains is our inner image remembered, the shadow of our true self. What will people put on your weather beaten shingle?

OUR PRAYER: *Master, please help me to leave a legacy of goodness and service to my fellow men and women. Let them see you through me. Amen.*

OUR SCRIPTURE: *"What is man that you think of him or the son of man that you care for him? You made him lower than the angels for a little while. You crowned him with glory and honor. You put all things under his control."*
– Hebrews 2:6-8 (New English Translation)

On a British Airways flight from Johannesburg, a middle-aged, well-off white South African lady had found herself sitting next to a black man. She called the cabin crew attendant over to complain about her seating. "What seems to be the problem, Madam?" asked the attendant.

"Can't you see?" she said. "You've sat me next to a kaffir. I can't possibly sit next to this disgusting human. Find me another seat!" "Please calm down, Madam," the stewardess replied. "The flight is very full today, but I'll tell you what I'll do. I'll go and check if we have any seats available in club or first class." The woman cocked a snooty look at the outraged black man beside her (not to mention at many of the surrounding passengers).

A few minutes later, the stewardess returned with the good news which she delivered to the lady, who could not help but look at the people around her with a smug and self-satisfied grin: "Madam, unfortunately, as I suspected, economy is full. I've spoken to the cabin services director, and club is also full. However, we do have one seat in first class."

Before the lady had a chance to answer, the stewardess continued... "It is most extraordinary to make this kind of upgrade, however, and I have had to get special permission from the captain. But, given the circumstances, the captain felt that it was outrageous that someone be forced to sit next to such an obnoxious person." With which, she turned to the black man sitting next to her, and said: "So, if you'd like to get your things, sir, I have your seat ready in first class up at the front..." At which point, apparently the surrounding passengers stood and gave a standing ovation, while the gentleman walked up to first class in the front of the plane.

Continued on next page.

We smile and silently applaud. We feel disgusted and angry that someone would act that way toward another human being. But, let's do a check-up before we feel too good about ourselves. What was our reaction to a young mother wrestling with several small children in the store? What was our reaction to that person whose clothes were shabby or ill-fitted? What was our reaction to the family speaking in another language, other than English, having a hard time being understood? What was our reaction to the man or woman trying to find the right change at the cash register, while we were in a hurry? What was our reaction to the new clerk in the store, who didn't know the merchandise?

I don't know about you, but I am suddenly not feeling so perfect.

OUR PRAYER: *Master, humble me to look upon others as your children, loved by you, as I am loved by you. Then, help me to reach out on your behalf. Amen.*

OUR SCRIPTURE: *"Never walk away from someone who deserves help; your hand is God's hand for that person. Don't tell your neighbor, 'Maybe some other time,' or, 'Try me tomorrow,' when the money's right there in your pocket. Don't figure ways of taking advantage of your neighbor when he's sitting there trusting and unsuspecting."*
– Proverbs 3:27-29 (The Message)

Recently, I was gazing through a newspaper and came across one of those "believe it or not" stories I had to share.

It's about Jim Davis, a grocery store clerk who loves his job and prides himself on his good work. One of his pet peeves is out-of-control toddlers and parents who yell at their kids, but do nothing to correct their children's obnoxious behavior.

One evening, Jim was checking out a customer with a shopping cart full of groceries. While ringing up the sale, a child began screaming very loudly, and a man angrily responded, "Get down!"

What a jerk, thought Jim, without even looking up. He kept on calling out prices and moving the groceries past the scanner. The kid behind him was still crying, and again he heard the man yell, "Get down!" Sheesh. Talk about poor parenting, thought Jim. This guy is a total jerk. He kept on checking groceries without looking up.

Finally, finishing the customer's cart, Jim looked up and said, "That'll be $89.95, ma'am." Seeing no one, he looked around and noticed everyone, including his customer, was lying face down on the floor.

He turned around just in time to see a gunman leave the store. The checker behind him, still lying on the floor, calmly said, "Jim, you know the second time you heard 'Get down,' his gun was pointed right at your head."

Continued on next page.

Somehow, I feel Jim Davis and I must have a common blood line. I have been noted to be so focused on a book or TV show that I'm totally oblivious to the noise and activities around me. This works especially well when my wife wants me to do something. I know my kids have it down to an art.

We get so accustomed to the noise of our surroundings, and the chosen distractions, when we hear someone tell us something important, we blow it off as if it were not significant. We become locked in our inner world of routine, and even build the wall of apathy, to hide behind. We go on with business as usual.

At times, I have been jolted with reality, becoming aware of surprising things around me. At times, it was funny when I seemingly "woke up" from la-la land; but, other times it wasn't so funny. I was brought back to reality when my wife was not feeling well for a while. I was brought back to reality when my child had a hard time at school, or with friends. I was brought back to reality, encountering ordinary people around me, in stores, or in line somewhere.

"Business as usual" can be dangerous to both body and soul. We blind ourselves to the dangers of our world. Also, we blind ourselves to the needs of those we love and opportunities to make a difference in someone's life.

Today, I challenge you to look up from your seemingly "business as usual" day and see through God's eyes. Be alert to the dangers around you, but also for opportunities to do something special for someone. Instead of just an "$89.95" day, it might be worth a million.

OUR PRAYER: *Master, today a person will be in my midst whom I can help. Open my eyes, ears, and heart to truly see and hear them. Amen.*

EVEN THOUGH

OUR SCRIPTURE: *"Then he said, 'Do you understand what I have done to you? You address me as 'Teacher,' and 'Master,' and rightly so. That is what I am. So if I, the Master and Teacher, washed your feet, you must now wash each other's feet. I've laid down a pattern for you. What I've done, you do. I'm only pointing out the obvious. A servant is not ranked above his master; an employee doesn't give orders to the employer. If you understand what I'm telling you, act like it—and live a blessed life.'"* – John 13:12-17 (The Message)

Dear God,

Even though I lie here, dreading to crawl out of my bed to face another day, I thank you for a bed to lie upon and a night's rest. There are many here who sleep on the floor or who will never rise to greet another day.

Even though I gripe about not having the type of food I want, I thank you that I have enough food to eat. I see the people here in their poverty, wondering if they will have anything at all to eat.

Even though I complain about being deployed away from my family, I thank you for keeping them safe. I hear the sounds of war and watch the children without parents who are injured from disease, and mines, in a hostile land.

Even though I gripe about the dust and dirt, swirling in the wind, stinging my eyes, I thank you that I have sight. There are many here who see only darkness as a result of simple cataracts and preventable diseases.

Even though I grow weary of wearing the same uniform day after day, I thank you for enough clothing to keep me warm. I see families without shoes, gloves, and blankets.

Continued on next page.

Even though I gripe about so much paperwork, I thank you that I have the ability to read and write. I watch a child who is given a crayon or pencil for the first time and yearns to learn.

Even though I gripe, complain, and bemoan my fate, from day to day, and wish my circumstances were not so modest, I thank you, Lord, for life.

Amen.

OUR PRAYER: *Master, as I have prayed, I thank you Lord, for life. Amen.*

A LESSON IN WOLF HUNTING

OUR SCRIPTURE: *"Be brave. Be strong. Don't give up. Expect God to get here soon."* – Psalm 31:24 (The Message)

The Chinese symbol for the word "crisis" actually combines the two words "danger" and "opportunity." Now, don't ask me to write it out for you, but take my word for it. When we are surrounded by difficulties and challenges, we may, in fact, be surrounded by many opportunities. When we encounter a paralyzing crisis, we may choose to be frightened and cowardly, or strong and courageous, realizing victory is moments away. It's all a matter of perspective.

An organization in Montana offered a bounty of five thousand dollars for every wolf captured alive. Two hunters named Sam and Jed decided to head for the hills and make some quick money capturing wolves. After all, wolves are nothing but big dogs. Day and night, they searched for the valuable prey. Exhausted after three days, Sam suddenly woke up to find he and Jed were surrounded by a pack of fifty wolves, with flaming red eyes and bared teeth, snarling and ready to pounce.

Sam nudged Jed and said, "Hey, wake up! We're gonna be rich!"

It's hard to see opportunity when you feel stress, doubt, fear, anger or depression. During a crisis, or crises, this is how we feel. Opportunity knocking is drowned out by the banging of defeat. These feelings drain our optimism, our clear vision and wholesome good. We don't see opportunity, except in being chewed up and eaten by the crisis. It's more a matter of teaching ourselves a different perspective before the crisis.

Sam may have been a bit overly optimistic, but he had the idea. I bet many of his other crises were met with accomplishment, rather than defeat. He looked at opportunity first. We can do the same, and we have to be patient. It may take a while to change a lifetime habit of wrong perspective, but God is ready to help us.

OUR PRAYER: *Master, today, and each day, will offer opportunities beyond my imagination to make a difference and truly live. I seek you in showing me those moments. Amen.*

IT'S THE LITTLE THINGS

OUR SCRIPTURE: *"Jesus went on to make these comments: If you're honest in small things, you'll be honest in big things; if you're a crook in small things, you'll be a crook in big things. If you're not honest in small jobs, who will put you in charge of the store? No worker can serve two bosses: He'll either hate the first and love the second or adore the first and despise the second. You can't serve both God and the Bank."*
– Luke 16:10-13 (The Message)

I could taste the steaks grilling. With some really good imagination, I could even smell them. I was salivating and couldn't wait to finish putting the grill together. There were about five bags of different size nuts, bolts, washers, plastic thing-a-ma-jigs, and a large sheet of step-by-step instructions in three languages. No problem!

At the end of the hour long jigsaw puzzle of parts, I was about done putting on the wheels. Then I saw it…a bolt, and nut, just lying there. Was it an extra in case of losing one? I soon found out.

The small bolt held a piece together and should have been used during step number three. I slowly began the process of dismantling the grill to begin step three all over again. About that time, my son came out and wanted to know when the steaks would be ready. He narrowly escaped with his life back into the house.

One lousy bolt, but the whole grill wouldn't function properly. If I had just paid attention to the little things of the grill, I wouldn't have messed up. Wait a minute! That also applies to a lot of things in our lives. If we pay attention to the seemingly little things in life, then the big, important things won't be weak and eventually lost. Here are a few other little things that could make a big difference:

- The bolt that holds the oil in the car

- The smile

- The hand on the shoulder

Continued on next page.

IT'S THE LITTLE THINGS

- The order for putting a barbeque grill together

- A single leaf floating down to join others

- A snowflake

- A moment of inspiration and encouragement, by being still and listening and seeing

- A flower among weeds

- A note of encouragement/love in a lunch bag or briefcase

- Holding hands

- A silent gaze into another's eyes

- Simple words and phrases that stand alone: Love you! I'm sorry. I missed you. I need you. I'm scared. Dad. Mom. Son. Daughter. Husband. Wife. Lover.

You may add more to your list. The little things done, one-by-one, can add up to something wonderful and powerful. The little things not done can undermine, and eventually, destroy something of great value and importance.

Pay attention to the little things today. If you do, you will notice they will add up to a big, blessed, wonderful day.

OUR PRAYER: *Master, the greater you become, the smaller my problems. With you by my side, nothing can defeat me. Allow me to see your greatness in both small, and big, moments of life. Amen.*

LOVELY LOOKS, ROTTEN TASTE

OUR SCRIPTURE: *"Mixed motives twist life into tangles; pure motives take you straight down the road."*
– Proverbs 21:8 (The Message)

It seems everyone around me is losing weight by extra exercise, changing eating habits, or not eating much at all. Anyway, I decided to get leaner and meaner with a better diet. The fruit here is delicious. I'm not sure where it comes from, but the pears are my favorite. The other day after exercising to get "beefier," I took a delicious looking pear for lunch. I momentarily eyed the pear, eagerly awaiting the sweetness soon to pass my lips. As I took a generous bite, I did not feel the usual crunch accompanying my partaking of this fruit. Instead, what I bit into was a mealy, mushy, rotten pear! What I expected to be sweet, white pear meat was, instead, bitter, brown, rotted flesh. I quickly looked around to get rid of this terrible taste, and luckily, I was in my office where no one could see me.

We are often fooled by people who, by their demeanor and good deeds, look good on the outside; but, we later find out the inside of their heart is less than sweet. We want people to be authentic and truthful, both inside and out.

Sadly, some people discover this after the wedding vows, after the votes are in, or after making a contribution to a cause based on first impressions. We are often fooled by outward looks and actions, we discover too late that under the skin, is only rotten fruit. Whose fault is it?

Maybe, we don't take the time to discern with our eyes, our hearts, our minds. We choose to be fooled. We choose blindness.

I wonder how many of us expect our inner being to be sweet and appealing, matching our outward appearance of good deeds and kind words. We need to look closely to what we portray, versus our inner character. Do our good deeds and actions reflect a caring heart and unselfishness? Do our words match our thoughts?

Continued on next page.

LOVELY LOOKS, ROTTEN TASTE

Look within yourself and make sure the lovely texture of what you display to the world matches what God has placed in your heart and soul. The Lord doesn't make rotten fruit; we are self-made people.

OUR PRAYER: *Master, please help me to be pure before you. Show me the cracks and dirt that I do not see, and give me the humility to make the changes you require. Amen.*

PEACEFUL SYMPTOMS

OUR SCRIPTURE: *"Blessed be God, who has given peace to his people Israel just as he said he'd do. Not one of all those good and wonderful words that he spoke through Moses has misfired. May God, our very own God, continue to be with us just as he was with our ancestors—may he never give up and walk out on us. May he keep us centered and devoted to him, following the life path he has cleared, watching the signposts, walking at the pace and rhythms he laid down for our ancestors."* – 1 Kings 8:56-58 (The Message)

There is a disease that isn't as well-known as some others, but knowledge of it is important to our health. This disease can imbed itself silently with huge effects. You need to be on the lookout for the symptoms that crop up. Be on guard. The disease is called "inner peace." Don't let it get you. Spread the word. Here are the symptoms. You need to be aware. You might want to post these on your refrigerator, or desk top:

- Tendency to think and act spontaneously, based on past experience.

- An unmistakable ability to enjoy each moment.

- Loss of interest in judging other people.

- Loss of interest in judging self.

- Loss of interest in interpreting the actions of others.

- Loss of ability to worry (very serious symptom).

- Frequent, overwhelming episodes of appreciation.

- Contented feelings of connectedness with God and others.

- Frequent attacks of smiling, through the eyes, and from the heart.

Continued on next page.

PEACEFUL SYMPTOMS

- Increasing tendency to let things happen, rather than make them happen.

- Increased susceptibility to receive love, as well as uncontrollable urges to extend love.

Yes, it does sound deadly. I know you don't want to catch such a disease. It would change your whole life, as well as those around you. Don't lose this way of life you have worked so hard to create. If this disease is left unchecked, you might begin to like who you are becoming and what you do…and enjoy living.

OUR PRAYER: *Master, my soul is at peace, knowing you are in control and have all power. To know I am in your will brings me comfort and joy. Amen.*

THE RIGHT QUESTION

OUR SCRIPTURE: *"Make the Master proud of you by being good citizens. Respect the authorities, whatever their level; they are God's emissaries for keeping order. It is God's will that by doing good, you might cure the ignorance of the fools who think you're a danger to society. Exercise your freedom by serving God, not by breaking the rules. Treat everyone you meet with dignity. Love your spiritual family. Revere God. Respect the government."* – 1 Peter 2:13-17 (The Message)

I found this prayer in my files. It is very insightful, so I want to share it with you. Think carefully about what it says to you regarding your responsibility and the Master's:

I asked God to take away my habit.
God said, "No. It is not for me to take away, but for you to give it up."

I asked God to make my handicapped child whole.
God said, "No. His spirit is whole, his body is only temporary."

I asked God to grant me patience.
God said, "No. Patience is a byproduct of tribulations; it isn't granted, it is learned."

I asked God to give me happiness.
God said, "No. I give you blessings; happiness is up to you."

I asked God to spare me pain.
God said, "No. Suffering draws you apart from worldly cares and brings you closer to me."

I asked God to make my spirit grow.
God said, "No. You must grow on your own. But, I will prune you to make you fruitful."

Continued on next page.

THE RIGHT QUESTION

I asked God for all things that I might enjoy life.
God said, "No. I will give you life, so you may enjoy all things."

I asked God to help me LOVE others, as much as He loves me.
God said...Ahhhh, finally you have the idea.

OUR PRAYER: *Master, I now get it. Thank you for not answering my prayers according to my agenda. Help me to love as you love. Amen.*

FILLING THE EMPTINESS

OUR SCRIPTURE: *"Summing up: Be agreeable, be sympathetic, be loving, be compassionate, be humble. That goes for all of you, no exceptions. No retaliation. No sharp-tongued sarcasm. Instead, bless—that's your job, to bless. You'll be a blessing and also get a blessing. Whoever wants to embrace life and see the day fill up with good, here's what you do: say nothing evil or hurtful; snub evil and cultivate good; run after peace for all you're worth. God looks on all this with approval, listening and responding well to what he's asked; but he turns his back on those who do evil things."* **– 1 Peter 3:8-12 (The Message)**

What do these four anecdotes have in common?

1. I had a taste for a cold diet soda. I took one out of the refrigerator and popped the top. I could already taste the effervescent soda lubricating my dry throat. I took a healthy gulp and immediately made a bad face of disgust. It had no effervescence and was syrupy bland. Yuuuk! I immediately threw it away.

2. The other day, a book title looked interesting It was soon apparent I didn't like the story and wasn't interested.
   So, I got rid of it.

3. Recently, I threw a shirt away. It had changed colors, faded, had holes, and had shrunk to an uncomfortable size. It wasn't good to wear any longer, so it was of no use to me.

4. A little girl went up to her mother one day while holding her stomach saying, "Mommy, my stomach hurts."

Her mother replied, "That's because it's empty. You have to put something into it!" She then prepared a bowl of soup.

Continued on next page.

Later that day, the chaplain came over for dinner. The chaplain began to feel badly. Holding his head, he said, "I have such a terrible headache!" The little girl looked up at him, giving him the sweetest smile any little child could give. Then, she said, "That's because it's empty. You have to put something into it!"

That last line above held the biggest clue. When something isn't right for you, get rid of it. When something doesn't fit into your life and causes discomfort, throw it away. You should be very discreet and demanding when placing things into your life. When you need love, choose someone capable of love. When you need support, pick the best. When you need knowledge, read and listen to quality knowledge. When you have a shortage of faith, look to God's Word. When you need to fill an emptiness in your life, be careful how you fill that void. It will change your life forever. You have no choice whether to fill the emptiness or not. If there is emptiness, it will be filled; but, with what? You decide.

OUR PRAYER: *Master, fill my heart and soul with joy in living. Fill my mind with knowledge of your will and direction. Fill me, Lord. Amen.*

OUR SCRIPTURE: *"The serpent told the woman, "You won't die. God knows that the moment you eat from that tree, you'll see what's really going on. You'll be just like God, knowing everything, ranging all the way from good to evil."*
– Genesis 3:4-5 (The Message)

"He who fights with monsters might take care lest he thereby become a monster.

And if you gaze for long into an abyss, the abyss gazes also into you."
–Friedrich Nietzsche

I have crept slowly, as well as run blindly, toward my abysses. I seek to see if I'm strong enough to withstand the ugly depth that seemingly draws me to its edge. I laughingly dance along the edge to flaunt my nimbleness and power. But, like the Siren of the Rocks, the abyss calls me to take one more step; take one more look. The lie is softly and subtly whispered in my ear, "There is no danger." I convince myself that I have the power to resist destruction.

I return to the edge and gaze into its evil depths, listening to its call to let go and resist no more. There, through the mist, I see something that startles me. I see my weaknesses. I see my hypocrisy. I see my shameful, secret yearnings. I see the ugliness within me that I deny. I grow cold and afraid.

I close my eyes to this monster that resembles me. I turn my back and resist with bold, decisive change. I run from the danger, wild-eyed and fearful. I race into the arms of God. I then rest and look around. I now have peace. I now see the beauty that surrounds me. My fears are gone. The abyss is a memory, an experience, and a turning point. I rise up and continue on, knowing another abyss may be over the next hill. What will I do? I will remember my victory, through God, and continue on in hope and faith.

OUR PRAYER: *Master, hold my hand, guide me. Keep me safe from myself and my selfish ways. Pull me from the abyss and draw me closer to you. You are my rock. Amen.*

OUR SCRIPTURE: *"During the meal, Jesus took and blessed the bread, broke it, and gave it to his disciples: 'Take, eat. This is my body.' Taking the cup and thanking God, he gave it to them: "Drink this, all of you. This is my blood, God's new covenant poured out for many people for the forgiveness of sins. I'll not be drinking wine from this cup again until that new day when I'll drink with you in the kingdom of my Father."*
– Matthew 26:26-29 (The Message)

"I may forgive, but I'll never forget." Ever heard that statement before? I have, from my own lips. I not only said it several times, but have lived up to it. What I really meant was I'll never forget, and will eventually get even. It is so hard to forgive. So hard to let the past be the past.

It is like the elderly Virginian woman who lived to see her beloved Richmond occupied by Union troops after the American Civil War. While walking down a Richmond street, she tripped over a step and fell. A Union soldier courteously helped her up.

"How very kind of you, young man," she said acidly. "If there is a cool spot in hell, I hope you get it."

Wow! She was just a tad unforgiving. However, come to think about it, I've made similar comments myself, on occasion. At least my attitude has been the same.

A beautiful legend tells of an African tribe that ritualizes forgiveness. When a tribe member acts irresponsibly or unjustly, he/she is taken to the center of the village. All work ceases and every man, woman and child in the village gathers in a large circle around the accused. Then, the tribe bombards the rejected person with affirmations! One at a time, friends and family enumerate all the good the individual has done. Every incident, every experience that can be recalled, with some detail and accuracy, is recounted. All their positive attributes, strengths and kindnesses are recited carefully and at length. Finally, the tribal circle is broken, a joyous celebration takes place, and the outcast is welcomed back into the tribe.

Continued on next page.

Forgiveness does not change the past. We must still live with the memory. It is what we do with the memory, and future actions, that make the difference. It is an inspiring picture to witness friendships and love restored through forgiveness. I've seen marriage partners look into each other's eyes, acknowledge the pain and hurt, and give the gift of forgiveness to begin anew. It wasn't easy, but something wonderful and miraculous usually isn't.

That is really the issue. We need to replace hurt with happiness, pain with peace. Rejection is now restored to wholeness. Where are the rejections in your life? Is there a heavy weight of hurt, anger, and no forgiveness? Your Lord forgives you. That's a perfectly good start.

OUR PRAYER: *Master and author of true forgiveness, help me to be like you. I find it hard to let go of the anger and vengeful thoughts. Remind me that because you forgave me, then I am able to forgive others. Amen.*

OUR SCRIPTURE: *"Don't hit back; discover beauty in everyone. If you've got it in you, get along with everybody. Don't insist on getting even; that's not for you to do. 'I'll do the judging,' says God. 'I'll take care of it.'"* **– Romans 12:17-18 (The Message)**

John was driving home late one night when he picked up a hitchhiker. As they rode along, he began to be suspicious of his passenger. John checked to see if his wallet was safe in the pocket of his coat that was on the seat between them, but it wasn't there! So he slammed on the brakes, ordered the hitchhiker out, and said. "Hand over the wallet immediately!" The frightened hitchhiker handed over a billfold, and John drove off. When he arrived home, he started to tell his wife about the experience, but she interrupted him, saying, "Before I forget, John, do you know that you left your wallet at home this morning?"

How many quick judgments have you made, only to learn you were terribly wrong? I sadly confess those moments in my life. I see someone looking lowly, destitute and lazy, but after speaking to them, or hearing more about them, I find just the opposite. However, I had already pushed them aside with a judgment.

Have you quickly judged someone as a wrongdoer, only to find out they were the victim? You were embarrassed, weren't you? We often judge too quickly based on words said, gestures given and appearances. You remember being wrongly judged, don't you? Didn't feel too good, did it?

What bothers me even more is that I don't judge myself as quickly as I judge others. I find excuses for what I do. I judge people down, while judging myself up. Is the answer to judge all up, and allow them to bring themselves down on their own merits? I just might be surprised how good people are, if given the chance…even myself.

OUR PRAYER: *Master, judge me according to your mercies and grace. Please don't judge me according to what I deserve. Then, help me to judge others likewise. Amen.*

OUR SCRIPTURE: *"Rash language cuts and maims, but there is healing in the words of the wise."*
– Proverbs 12:18 (The Message)

A woman came into the doctor's office and complained about having severe pain at several spots on her body. The doctor asked where they were. She touched her knee and yelled in pain. She touched her neck and screamed again in pain. She then touched her side and jumped in pain. The doctor then told her to sit still as he examined her. After several moments, he said that he found the problem. She had a broken finger.

No one wants to have a sore spot touched, and likewise a society or community with many sores will twitch when someone has the courage to touch one and say: "You have to treat that. You have to get rid of that." Those who do point out where the sore spots are in an individual or community aren't always popular. But, it needs to be done. It takes care, wrapped up in courage, to step forward and show brokenness and pain. We need to touch one another in love where it hurts to reveal what needs to be healed.

The diagnosis is in. There is hurt, brokenness, disease, and fractures in our fallen world. You can see and hear the symptoms. Do you have the courage to touch another with God's love and reveal where there is the need for healing? If not you, then who will? Waiting just allows pain to continue. Help your friends and loved ones. Touch them where they need it the most in order for healing to take place.

OUR PRAYER: *Master, as you have healed my body and spirit, allow me to likewise reach out to those I meet in your name. Amen.*

JUST A BIT MORE

OUR SCRIPTURE: *"Because of the Master, we have great confidence in you. We know you're doing everything we told you and will continue doing it. May the Master take you by the hand and lead you along the path of God's love and Christ's endurance." – 2 Thessalonians 3:4-5 (The Message)*

It didn't take much more, but at the moment, it seemed beyond my strength. With grunts and red-faced surges, I used all my strength to no avail. Then, with one more supreme effort, I tried again and won! Finally, the lid to the jar of salsa popped opened.

With enough persistence, tiny, soft water droplets will wear away the hardest stone. With persistence, a small seed can grow into a towering tree. With persistence, anyone can make a difference.

With persistence, one small effort builds on top of the one before, until the combined force is undeniable. Small, focused efforts, strung together over time with persistence and determination, bring about magnificent results.

So much effort is wasted because it is spent against itself. In our impatience, we zigzag off in so many different directions and end up covering very little ground. Only by focused persistence can we reliably and consistently make progress, and maximize our efforts.

Where do you want to go? Who do you want to be? What do you want to accomplish? What possibilities is God waiting for you to fulfill? Could it be your marriage, your job, a relationship with a child, or a task that seems monumental, even insurmountable? Often, it only takes one more effort. Do not give up too soon. Persistence pays off.

OUR PRAYER: *Master, my strength is limited, but your strength knows no bounds. Humble me to rely on your strength when mine gives out. Amen.*

ID TEN T ERRORS

OUR SCRIPTURE: *"God alone knows the way to Wisdom, he knows the exact place to find it. He knows where everything is on earth, he sees everything under heaven. After he commanded the winds to blow and measured out the waters, arranged for the rain and set off explosions of thunder and lightning, he focused on Wisdom, made sure it was all set and tested and ready. Then, he addressed the human race: 'Here it is! Fear-of-the-Lord—that's Wisdom, and insight means shunning evil.'"* – Job 28:23-28 (The Message)

Sometimes, I feel so stupid. Like the other night, I looked all over for the detergent to wash my clothes. I pushed things aside in the locker where I always keep it. I took things out. I finally concluded I had left it in the laundry room, so I trucked down the hallway only to find it wasn't there. I knew I had it just the other day. So, I went back to the locker and pushed everything to the other side of the locker shelves and still didn't see it. All of the sudden, there it was right on the front of the shelf where I always keep it. Now, who put it there while I was gone down the hallway? It had to be a gremlin. I wouldn't be that stupid. I sound like this guy.

A man was having trouble with his computer. So, he called Bob-the-computer-guy, to come over. Bob clicked a couple of buttons and solved the problem. He gave the customer a bill for a minimum service call.

As he was walking away, the customer called after him, "So, what was wrong?" Bob replied, "It was an ID ten T error."

The customer didn't want to appear stupid, but nonetheless inquired, "An, ID ten T error? What's that, in case I need to fix it again?"

The computer guy grinned.... "Haven't you ever heard of an ID ten T error before?"

Continued on next page.

ID TEN T ERRORS

"No," the customer replied.

"Write it down," Bob said, "and I think you'll figure it out."

So the confused man wrote out....I D 1 0 T

The customer never called Bob again.

The obvious seems, many times, to be harder to see than the larger problems in life. Why? I guess partly because we take them for granted. The obvious is too obvious. The trees obstruct the view of the forest. We may be blinded to something right under our noses. When the person who lives with us is gone, we notice. When a child grows up and leaves home, we notice. When a person we care about doesn't return the love we feel and express, we notice. The obvious can be revealingly obvious when it's gone.

Right in front of you is someone who loves you. Right in front of you are opportunities to find joy and peace. Right in front of you are parents who have sacrificed for you. Right in front of you are friends who hang in there, always available to help, even at four a.m. Right in front of you is an opportunity to change someone's life for the better. Right in front of you is a God who never leaves your side, awaiting your love.

Don't do the ID ten T errors. Open your eyes and see what is right in front of you.

OUR PRAYER: *Master, open my eyes like you did for Job. Let me see how great and wise you are. Humble me from my pride and arrogance to know you are God. Amen.*

TEARS FROM AN OAK TREE

OUR SCRIPTURE: *"Now Peter got really nervous and swore, 'I never laid eyes on this man you're talking about.' Just then the rooster crowed a second time. Peter remembered how Jesus had said, 'Before a rooster crows twice, you'll deny me three times.' He collapsed in tears."* – Mark 14:71-72 (The Message)

It was a chilly day, as winter began it's time to make changes. This day a man, his heart heavy with grief, was walking in the woods. As he thought about his life this day, he knew many things were not right. He thought about those who had lied about him back when he had a job. His thoughts turned to those who had stolen his things and cheated him. He remembered family that had passed on. His mind turned to the illness he had that no one could cure. He saw the world of selfishness and greed. His very soul was filled with anger, resentment and frustration.

Standing there this day, searching for answers he could not find, knowing all else had failed him; he knelt at the base of an old oak tree searching for answers that wouldn't seem to come. His heart turned to the One whom he knew would always be there, and with tears in his eyes, he prayed, "Lord, you have done wonderful things for me in this life. You have told me to do many things for you, and I happily obeyed. Today, you have told me to forgive. I am sad, Lord, because I cannot. I don't know how. It is not fair, Lord. I didn't deserve these wrongs done against me and I shouldn't have to forgive. Lord, this one thing I cannot do, for I don't know how to forgive. My anger is so deep, Lord, I fear I may not hear you, but I pray you will teach me to do this one thing I cannot do. Teach me to FORGIVE."

As he knelt there in the quiet shade of that old oak tree, he felt something fall onto his shoulder. He opened his eyes. Out of the corner of one eye, he saw a leaf that had turned brown. He gazed upward and noted all the leaves turning colors and one by one softly falling to earth. They seemed like tears. He stood and looked at the trunk of the magnificent oak. There he saw scars, some deep and some shallow, marking its bark. He noted the twisting of the bark as well as the limbs

Continued on next page.

which shown the ravages of weather and time. Yet, the oak stood with its scars, standing tall, year after year, strong and getting stronger. On the trunk, he noted names chiseled with a pocket knife of two lovers. How that must have hurt the old oak!

Then, the man heard a voice speak to him. Have you ever told a lie, the Master asked? The man answered, "Yes, Lord." Have you ever been given too much change and kept it? The man answered, "Yes, Lord." And, the man sobbed more and more.

Have you ever taken something from work that wasn't yours, the Master asked? The man answered, "Yes, Lord."

Have you ever sworn, using my name in vain? The man, crying now, answered, "Yes, Lord."

As the Master asked many more times, "Have you ever?" The man's crying became uncontrollable, for he could only answer, "Yes, Lord."

Then, the man felt something again fall on his other shoulder. He looked and saw that it was another leaf, then another. The Master said each leaf was like a tear from the oak tree, sharing its hurts, pains, but most of all, life. The tree didn't deserve its scars either, but it forgave and continued to live.

The man reached out and touched the scars of the tree. He gazed upward to the twisted limbs, stretching outward. He felt the leaves of tears falling upon his face. Then, he knew what he could and must do…forgive, for he was forgiven. As the tears fell from the tree, so the tears of forgiveness and humility fell from the face of the man upon the earth.

OUR PRAYER: *Master, my heart breaks, and my tears flow, when I think of what I have done in shame. But you, Lord, reach down into my heart and make it clean. I do not deserve it, but you do it, anyway, because you love me. Thank you.*

THINGS I LEARNED BETWEEN 2:30–6:30 A.M.

OUR SCRIPTURE: *"God delights in concealing things; scientists delight in discovering things."* – Proverbs 25:2 (The Message)

Recently, I had to return to the United States on some family business. Now, keep in mind I am eleven hours ahead by time zone, from Texas. The jet lag reached a whole new dimension when I flew back. At 2 A.M., my eyes flew open and I found myself ready to start the day, whether my body agreed or not. Anyway, I got out of bed, made some coffee, and went to sit on the back patio, so I wouldn't wake up the normal people.

As I sat there, in the still night, I sipped my coffee and quietly looked around at this time of a day in which I normally don't participate. It was a magical time. I didn't want to begin the planning of the day or review of yesterday. I just wanted to be still. I began using all my senses, absorbing the night. I heard distant dogs barking, communicating in a language only dogs know. I heard the crickets, night birds, and other creatures, sharing the night together with me. I then looked up into the night sky, saw the stars shining down, with the half-moon hanging nearby. Wisps of clouds drifted by, on their way somewhere to possibly join up with others for rain.

As the dawn grew nearer, the stars began to disappear from my view, their light being taken over by the upcoming sun. Oddly, on the horizon, where there were no stars earlier, one star appeared and grew brighter as the sun began its shift. The star had been there all along, but I didn't see it until that certain time each morning. These are the things I saw each morning. Here are the things I learned:

Continued on next page.

THINGS I LEARNED BETWEEN
2:30—6:30 A.M.

1. The stars shine their brightest for our view at night, but are always there no matter the time of day. I have hidden the important things in my life. They are hidden from my view by the tasks at hand and living the day. You can call them my stars: the love of my family, my inner spiritual faith, the depth of my strength and endurance against obstacles, the ability to forgive, and a larger quantity of patience. They are not always in view until those certain times when needed. It is then, they are most clearly seen.

2. I discovered, like the one star shining just before the dawn, that God is there to show me the way before the dawn of life's challenges. Even when the day becomes bright and full, he is always there, pointing the way.

3. Finally, I learned I am negligent in discovering these opportunities, or, at least, keeping them alive in my thoughts and beliefs. I rush, trying to handle everything myself, taking for granted the hidden secrets of what life is really all about. I need to take time to hear, see, and feel all of life even when it seems hidden.

These are some things I learned between 2:30 and 6:30 A.M. I am not alone and life is good.

OUR PRAYER: *Master, the things I do not see and the things I do not understand are in your hands. You are God, above all gods, and Lord, above all lords. Amen.*